Prehistoric Flying Giants

by Monica Hughes

Consultant: Dougal Dixon

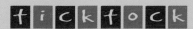

CONTENTS

Words in **bold** are explained in the glossary.

Very old animals

These **prehistoric** animals lived long before dinosaurs.

Coelurosauravus
see-lo-ro-sor-a-vus

This one looked like a lizard with wings.

This one looked like a dragonfly,
but was the size of a seagull.

Meganeura
meg-an-ura

The pterosaurs

The **pterosaurs** lived at the time of the dinosaurs.

They were big flying animals.

Pterosaur
terr-o-sor

Some of them had long tails and narrow wings.

Some had short tails and wide wings.

Narrow wings

This pterosaur had narrow wings and a long tail.

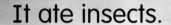

It ate insects.

Insect

It had a furry body.

Sordes
sor-dees

Furry body

This pterosaur was one metre from **wing tip** to wing tip.

It had a furry body.

It had a long tail.

Eudimorphodon
you-dee-morf-o-don

It had two kinds of
teeth.

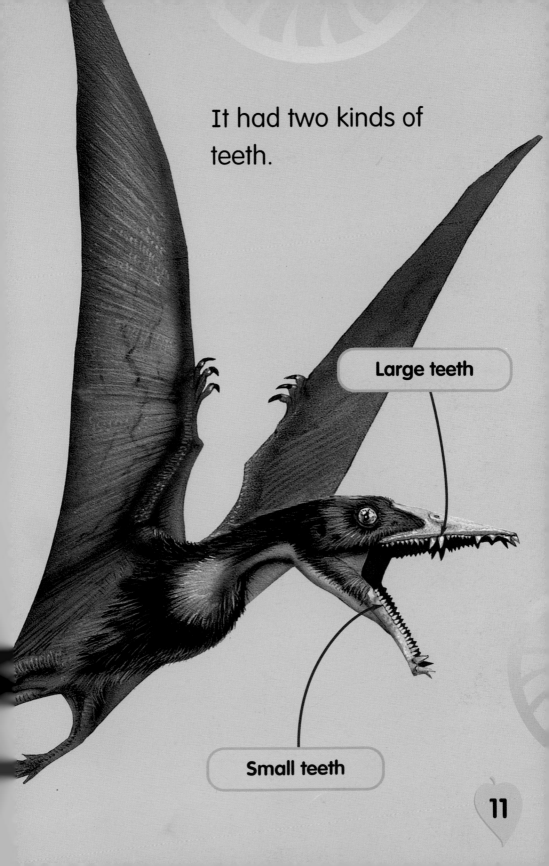

Large teeth

Small teeth

Big head

This pterosaur had a long tail and narrow wings.

Dimorphodon
die-morf-o-don

It ate fish.

Fish

It had a very big head and
a colourful beak.

13

Short tail

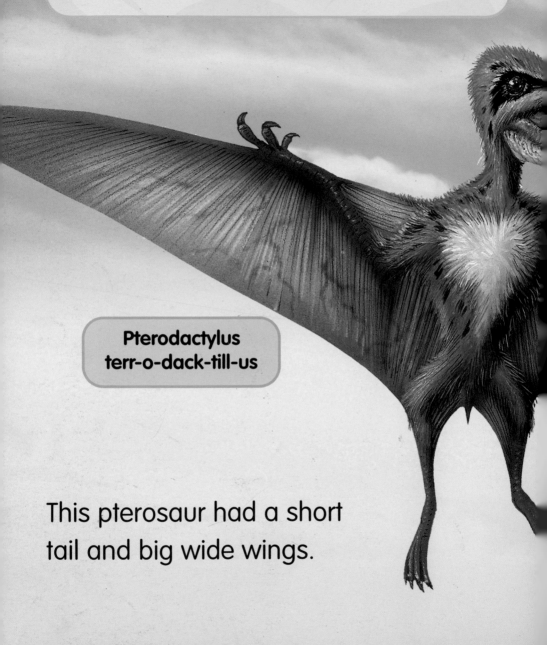

Pterodactylus
terr-o-dack-till-us

This pterosaur had a short
tail and big wide wings.

It ate fish and
small lizards.

Lizard

Colourful crest

This pterosaur was three metres from wing tip to wing tip.

It had pointed **jaws** to eat shellfish.

Shellfish

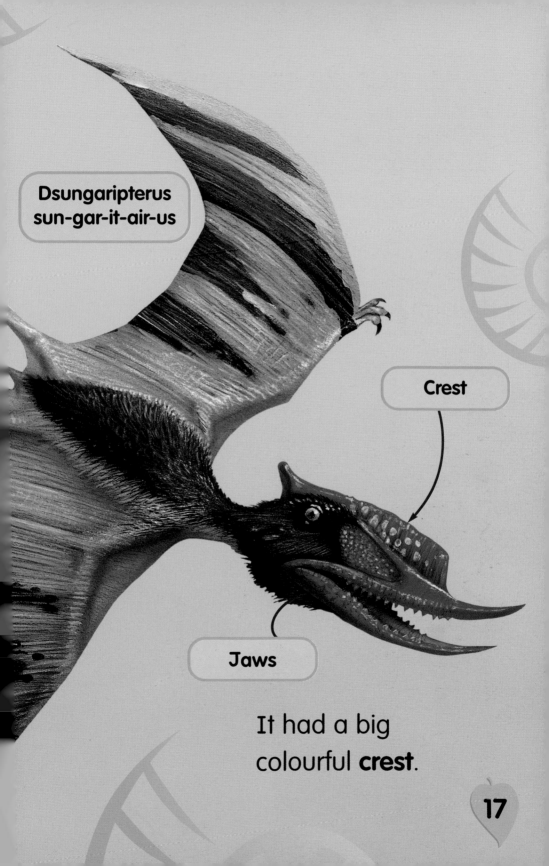

Dsungaripterus
sun-gar-it-air-us

Crest

Jaws

It had a big
colourful **crest**.

17

As big as an aeroplane

This pterosaur was the size of a small aeroplane.

It had a long neck and long jaws.

It ate dead dinosaurs.

Quetzalcoatlus
ket-sal-koat-lus

The first bird

This may have been the first bird.

It had feathers like a bird.

Archaeopteryx
ark-ee-op-ter-ix

Instead of a beak,
it had jaws and teeth.

21

Glossary

crest

A crown of skin on the top of the head.

jaws

The part of the skull that holds the teeth.

22

prehistoric
The millions of
years before
human history.

pterosaur
A flying animal
living at the
time of the
dinosaurs.

wing tip
The very end of
a wing.

Index

Copyright © ticktock Entertainment Ltd 2008
First published in Great Britain in 2008 by ticktock Media Ltd.,
Unit 2, Orchard Business Centre, North Farm Road, Tunbridge Wells, Kent TN2 3XF
ISBN 978 1 84696 753 5 pbk
Printed in China

We would like to thank: Penny Worms, Shirley Bickler, Suzanne Baker and the National Literacy Trust.

Picture credits (t=top, b=bottom, c=centre, l-left, r=right, OFC= outside front cover)
Lisa Alderson: 8-9, 12b; Simon Mendez: 4, 5, 12t; NHM: 6; Shutterstock: 8, 12, 15b, 16, 23b; Luis Rey: 1, 6-7, 10-11, 14-15, 17, 18-19, 20, 21, , 22t, 22b, 23t, 23c.